THE POWERFUL TRICERATOPS

BY PETER FINN

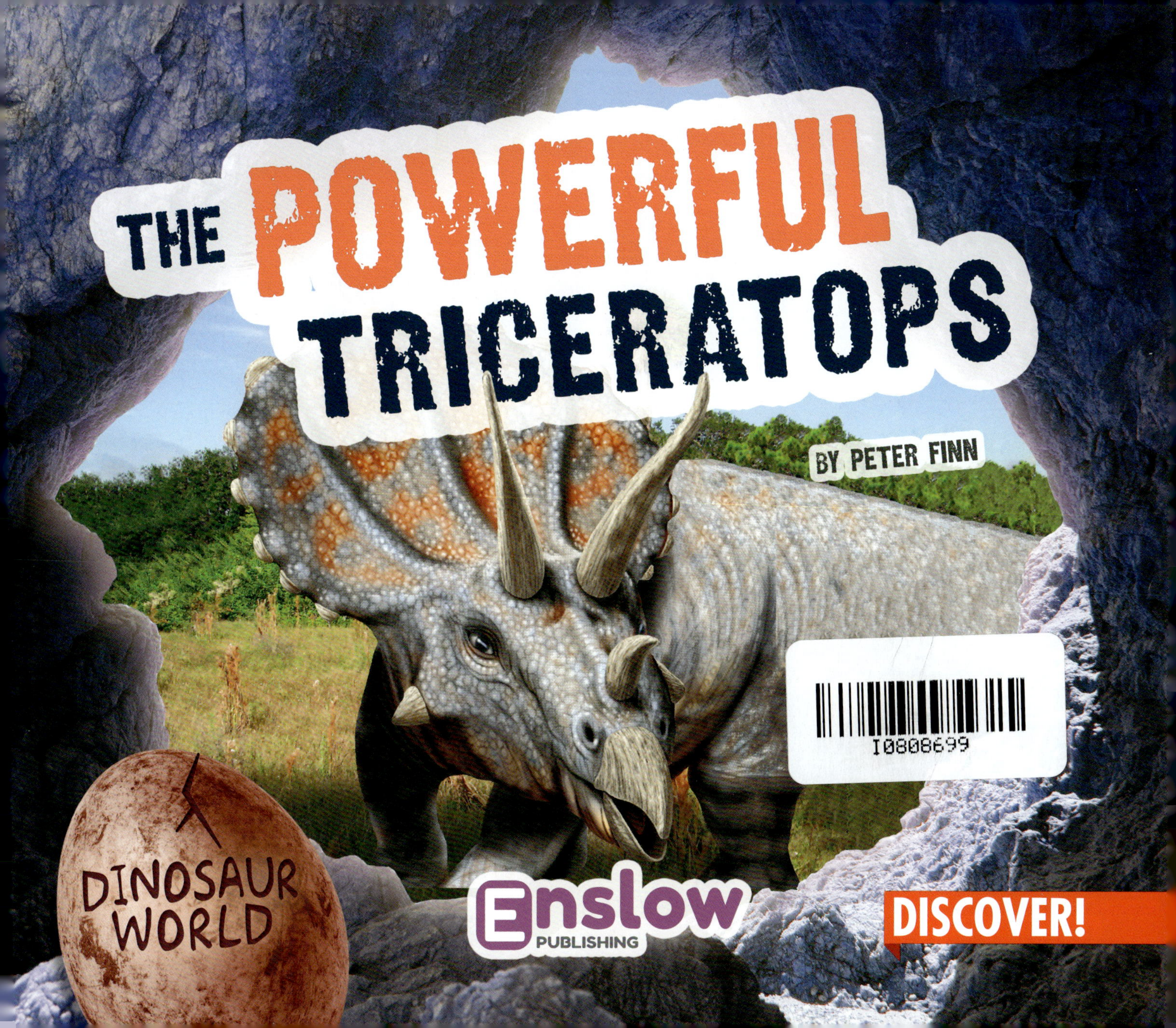

DINOSAUR WORLD

Enslow PUBLISHING

DISCOVER!

Library of Congress Cataloging-in-Publication Data

Names: Finn, Peter, 1978- author.
Title: The powerful triceratops / Peter Finn.
Description: New York : Enslow Publishing, [2022] | Series: Dinosaur world | Includes index.
Identifiers: LCCN 2020049663 (print) | LCCN 2020049664 (ebook) | ISBN 9781978521209 (library binding) | ISBN 9781978521186 (paperback) | ISBN 9781978521193 (set) | ISBN 9781978521216 (ebook)
Subjects: LCSH: Triceratops–Juvenile literature.
Classification: LCC QE862.O65 F56 2022 (print) | LCC QE862.O65 (ebook) | DDC 567.915/8-dc23
LC record available at https://lccn.loc.gov/2020049663
LC ebook record available at https://lccn.loc.gov/2020049664

Published in 2022 by
Enslow Publishing
101 West 23rd Street, Suite #240
New York, NY 10011

Designer: Sarah Liddell
Interior Layout: Rachel Rising
Editor: Therese Shea

Illustrations by Jeffrey Mangiat
Science Consultant: Philip J. Currie, Ph.D., Professor and Canada Research Chair of Dinosaur Palaeobiology at the University of Alberta, Canada

Photo credits: Cover, pp. 1, 5, 7, 9, 11, 13, 15, 17, 19, 21(rock border) SirinR/Shutterstock.com; pp. 4, 6, 8, 10, 12, 14, 16, 18, 20, 22, 23, 24 (background) altanaka/Shutterstock.com; pp. 5, 9, 11, 15, 19 (egg) fotoslaz/Shutterstock.com.

Portions of this work were originally authored by Daisy Allyn and published as Triceratops. All new material this edition authored by Peter Finn.

Printed in the United States of America

CONTENTS

Boldface words appear in Words to Know.

THREE HORNS

Triceratops was a large dinosaur. It lived more than 65 **million** years ago. Its name means "three-horned face." It had three sharp horns on its head. *Triceratops* was a plant eater. However, this dinosaur was good at **defending** itself from enemies!

HOW TO SAY *TRICERATOPS*:
TRY-SEHR-UH-TAHPS

SHARP WEAPONS

Triceratops had a horn above each eye. These horns could grow to be 3 feet (0.9 m) long. Another horn was on its **snout**. It was shorter. However, it was sharp too! These horns **protected** *Triceratops* against *Tyrannosaurus rex* (tie-RAN-uh-sore-us REX).

TYRANNOSAURUS
REX
THREE
HORNS

WHAT'S THE FRILL FOR?

Triceratops also had a frill. This was a bony body part on its neck. The frill might have protected the dinosaur against sharp teeth. It might have drawn **mates** to *Triceratops* too. Some scientists think the frill **released** body heat!

FRILL
WHAT DO YOU THINK
TRICERATOPS'S FRILL
WAS FOR?

BIG AND HEAVY

Triceratops was a bit larger than a big elephant. This dinosaur was about 30 feet (9 m) long. That's about as long as two cars. *Triceratops* weighed about 3 tons (4.5 mt). That's about the weight of three cars.

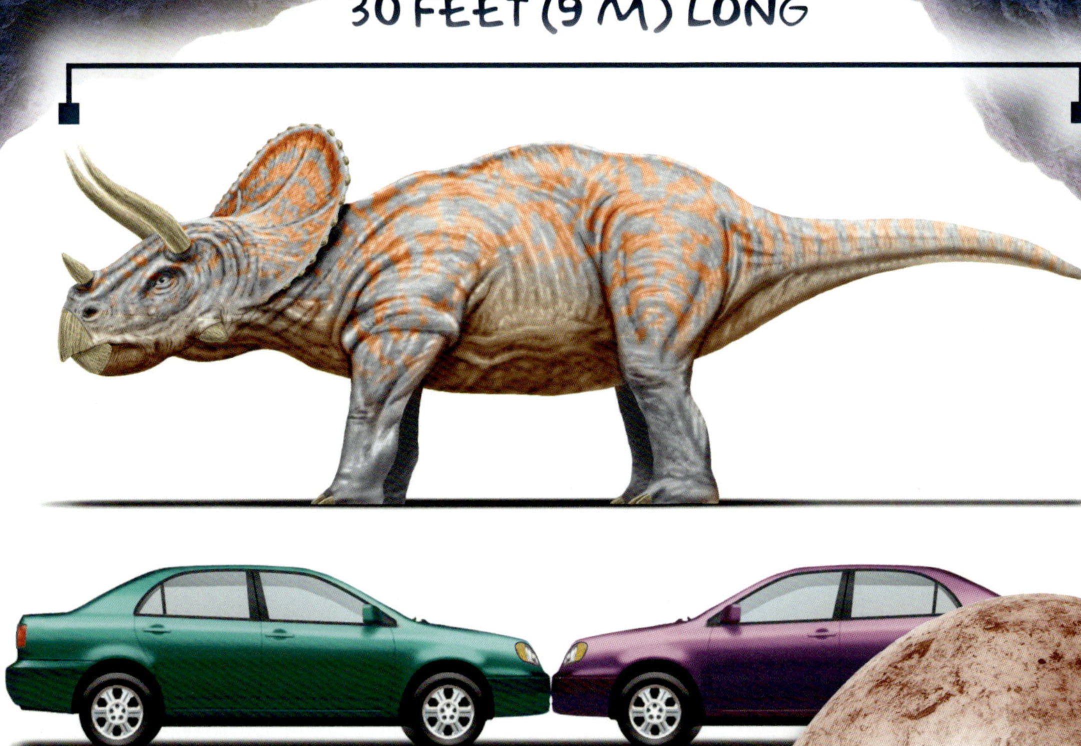

TRICERATOPS'S HEAD WAS ABOUT 6 FEET (1.8 M) LONG!

TOP SPEED

Triceratops walked on four legs. Its back legs were larger than its front legs. Its feet looked a bit like an elephant's feet. Because *Triceratops* was heavy, it wasn't fast. Its top speed was likely about 16 miles (26 km) per hour.

FASTEST SPEED = 16 MILES
(26 KM) PER HOUR

OUCH!

Triceratops was a dinosaur that could defend itself. How do we know it had **predators**? There are clues on **fossils** of *Triceratops*. For example, some *Triceratops* bones have bite marks that match the teeth of *Tyrannosaurus rex*!

SCIENTISTS THINK TYRANNOSAURS WERE THE MAIN PREDATOR OF *TRICERATOPS*.

BIG MEALS

Triceratops was an herbivore (HER-bih-vohr). That means it ate plants. It had a mouth like a **beak**. *Triceratops* had up to 800 teeth! These teeth were perfect for cutting and chewing tough plants. *Triceratops* ate plants that grew low to the ground.

UP TO
800 TEETH
BEAKLIKE
MOUTH

HERDS OR ALONE?

Scientists often find one *Triceratops* fossil at a time. However, fossils from a group of young *Triceratops* were discovered. That makes scientists think these young dinosaurs spent time together. They may have even lived in a herd.

SMALLER TRICERATOPS WOULD HAVE BEEN SAFER IN A HERD.

WHERE THEY LIVED

Triceratops fossils have only been found in North America. They were dug up in Montana, North Dakota, South Dakota, Colorado, and Wyoming. They've also been found in Saskatchewan and Alberta in Canada. There's more to discover about the tough *Triceratops*!

TRICERATOPS

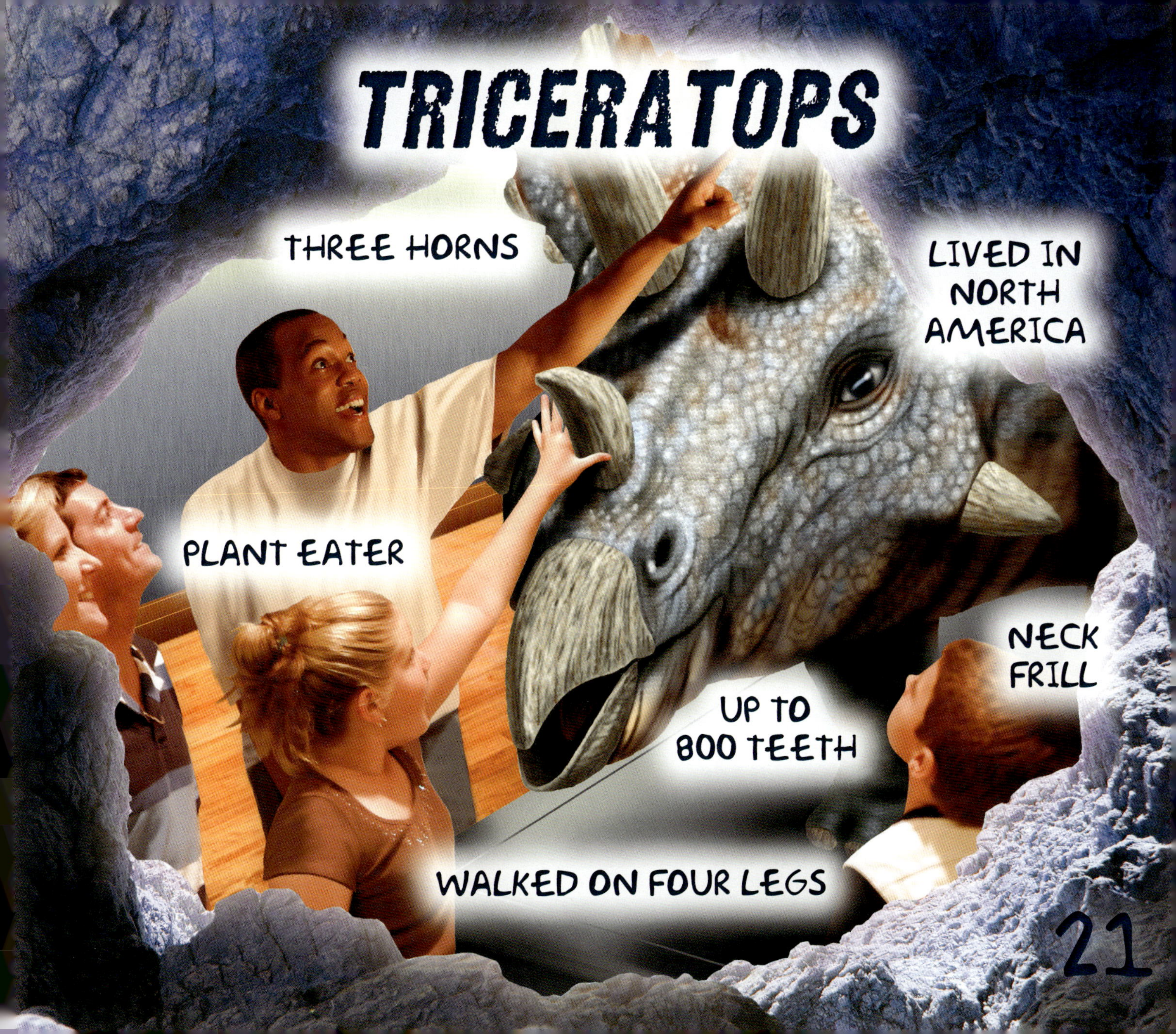

WORDS TO KNOW

beak A part of the mouth that sticks out on some animals and is used to tear food.

defend To guard against an enemy.

fossil The hardened marks or remains of plants and animals that formed over thousands or millions of years.

mate One of two animals that come together to produce babies.

million A thousand thousands, or 1,000,000.

predator An animal that hunts other animals for food.

protect To keep safe.

release To set something free.

snout An animal's nose and mouth.

FOR MORE INFORMATION

BOOKS

Carr, Aaron. *Triceratops*. New York, NY: AV2, 2021.

Nelson, Jake. *I'm a Triceratops*. Ann Arbor, MI: Cherry Lake, 2021.

Radley, Gail. *Triceratops*. Mankato, MN: Bolt, 2021.

WEBSITES

Triceratops
www.nhm.ac.uk/discover/dino-directory/triceratops.html
See how big this dinosaur was compared to a human.

***Triceratops* Facts for Kids**
www.sciencekids.co.nz/sciencefacts/dinosaurs/triceratops.html
Read some quick facts about *Triceratops*.

Publisher's note to educators and parents: Our editors have carefully reviewed these websites to ensure that they are suitable for students. Many websites change frequently, however, and we cannot guarantee that a site's future contents will continue to meet our high standards of quality and educational value. Be advised that students should be closely supervised whenever they access the internet.

INDEX